10

LITTLE RULES
for a
BLISSY LIFE

by Carol Pearson

ISBN-13: 978-0-9974799-0-4

For more information visit www.10littlerules.com

dedication

... to everyone who has lived,
learned and struggled to understand
the rules that really matter

... to Val and Jessie, for inspiring me to be
a better human, every single day

... to all my 10LRs sisters, for a hundred little reasons

... to Laurie, for seeing me through it all

... and to John, for reasons that continue to
unfold and surprise

table of contents

introduction

Growing up Irish Catholic in the 60s, I had a lot of rules to live by. Some made perfect sense. (Come home for dinner when you hear Mom blow the police whistle, or you'll go hungry.) Others not so much (no jeans to Mass on Sunday. This one I never understood be-cause our priest had a long red beard and wore sandals. I think he was channeling Jesus.) One of a brood of four, all close in age, I learned early that living by the rules meant staying under the radar, being the "good girl." I got good grades, got into a perfectly nice middle of the road Catholic college, and married the first guy I fell in love with.

Twenty-five years, two beautiful children and one pending divorce later, I found myself breaking every rule of common sense, happy home and responsible adulthood. Not because I hated my life; rather because I felt something much larger, more full of truth on the horizon, just beyond where my visible sight ended. I felt bottled up. I knew there had to be more. From all accounts, I was smack dab in the middle of a mid-life crisis.

Only it didn't feel like a crisis. It felt like breathing.

What I slowly began to realize is that I had been living my life to make everyone else happy, doing my best to follow the rules as they'd been laid out. I was living by the rules I thought I should follow, never asking for clarification or doing the tough work of evaluating them. In some ways, it was the easy path through life: less conflict, less guilt, and certainly a safer playing field. Yet what it provided in safety and comfort it lacked in passion and magic, two components I consider vital on my path to bliss.

I created magic where I could (our family's Tooth Fairy is the stuff of legends) and gave my all to creating a peaceful, loving home for my family. I had no real reason to be unhappy. Yet underneath, I felt an emptiness, a longing to experience life from my own point of view. I acted as if every decision had to be approved by the loud and highly critical committee in my head, constantly warning me of dire consequences waiting to descend if I dared listen to and honor my own voice.

I couldn't do it anymore.

So I rewrote my rule book, set my own compass for the next phase of my life. I am grateful for all the people in my life who gave me rules in the first place. This is not about blaming them for forcing me into a mold; I had free choice all along, I just never realized it. This is about finally seeing that my life is truly my own. I get to write my own rules, my own way of reacting to the world and determining my course. Now I get to live in radiant harmony with the thoughts of my own heart.

These 10 Little Rules work for me. I compiled them from a variety of sources, and some may already be familiar to you. You'll undoubtedly have your own rules for bliss, and I encourage you to write them down and make your own rule book. You'll find space throughout the book to jot down your own ideas and draft your own rules.

My hope is that you'll use this book to help you explore the things that truly matter to you, and recognize the ways in which your rules – real or imagined – are keeping you from true and profound happiness. Once you've discovered the rules that govern you, you can set about writing your own. And once you've done that and written your own rule book, you can own it, embrace it, and live your best #BlissyLife.

RULE #1
get to source

In our hyper-connected, goal-oriented world, the rush of things becomes a constant undercurrent to our day. How can we hear our hearts speaking their truth when there is so much noise and turbulence? Drowned out by the smartphone, social media, TV, neighbor, co-worker, spouse or child, the heart would have to scream to be heard.

In fact, my heart did scream. I found myself mired in a horrendous place, where I was close to violently unhappy in my situation. I was scared, vulnerable, and susceptible to quick fixes that only made things that much worse.

I began to recover when I spent some time each day in complete quiet. I didn't call it meditation at the time, just downtime. Eventually it grew into a practice of quietly learning to hear the voice of my heart, and really listening to what it said.

True healing began for me when I spent two months in a cottage on the Gulf of Mexico not quite a year after my divorce was final. I began every day with a four mile walk on the beach, with only the seagulls and an occasional dolphin to keep me company. With each step, I focused on clearing my head of the noise, the shouts and the chaos. Every step brought me closer to peace, until, finally, I arrived back at

RULE #1
get to source

at the cottage with a clear mind.

By the second month, I was introduced to a more formal meditation process, courtesy of the Chopra Center. Their 21-day meditation challenge was the perfect way for me to learn meditation and integrate it into my daily routine. The more I practiced this, the easier it became to block out the seemingly endless thoughts, the constant chorus of voices. And once I got to a place of quiet, I started to really hear my own voice, the voice of my own heart.

By the end of my two months on the shore, that quiet space turned into a new place for creativity and imagination, for problem-solving and forgiveness, and ultimately for a deep peace and joy that I had never known.

Eventually, I lost the habit of daily meditation. I was busy, happy building a new life and new relationships. I didn't make a conscious decision to stop; I just gradually stopped. I realized with a start one day that it had been several months since I meditated, and I could see an increase in my old anxiety issues and scattered thinking. I've started again, this time with the full realization of how powerful an act this is, and what a gift it is to myself and the people I spend time with.

You can find your source in so many places, in those little moments that take your breath away when you stand beside the ocean or on a mountaintop. For some, they find it in the garden, others while walking in the woods.

Sometimes our connection with our source comes totally out of the blue. I will never forget the moment I held my daughter Valerie for the first time. In that moment, I saw the Milky Way in her eyes, as if she knew all the wonders of the Universe. For the first time in my life, I felt completely connected to a presence much larger than myself. Call

RULE #1
get to source

it God, Creator, the Universe, Big Love…it is that ineffable oneness
that leads to understanding and peace.

This universal connection never really goes away; we just lose the
thread in the constant demands of our lives. And when we lose that,
how can we expect to understand ourselves, our place in the world and
what will truly make us happy and fill us with peace?

Begin today to find your source; just take 10 minutes and turn off
all the noise, breathe deeply and let the thoughts drift in and drift out
again. Focus on your breathing if you find yourself distracted by
thoughts. Tomorrow add another minute or two, breathing deeply and
relaxing. You can do this in meditation, in a long walk in the woods,
even sitting quietly on your porch in the sunshine.

For more formal help, look for information about meditation online,
take a yoga class, or spend some time in prayer. It doesn't take long to
build the habit, and I promise you the results will be amazing.

your turn ...

get to source

Where do you feel most connected, most able to hear your heart speak? What are your challenges or frustrations in getting to your true source? Use the journaling space on the following pages to write down your thoughts.

1

get to source

date _____

date _____

get to source

date _____

get to source

date _____

get to source

RULE #2
listen to your heart

Once I gave myself that clear space to be quiet and connect, I was amazed at what I heard. That tiny little voice I'd always sensed (but often couldn't make out) became clearer, stronger and more compelling. I realized with a start one day that this voice was my heart speaking.

We've all grown up hearing the platitudes of "listen to your heart" and "follow your bliss" yet how many of us experience the reality of this? Once my head quieted down, I was finally able to listen. The voice was unmistakable. There it was, letting me know what I wanted, how I truly felt about things, and where I was off track in my life. Once you connect with your heart's voice, then the fun begins. I won't kid you; this is also where a lot of pain can happen. What if you hear your voice, and realize that it's time to quit your job, leave your relationship, or drop a friendship that has turned toxic? What if that voice tells you something you've been denying about who you are and what you need out of life? What if your truth will hurt the people you love?

I still struggle with this idea. While it's easier now for me to hear the truth in my heart, I still sometimes find it a challenge to act on it. I've learned to be gentle with myself as I move toward my bliss.

RULE #2
listen to your heart

While some may be able to make that quantum leap in one moment, others will inch there, bit by bit. Forward motion is all that is required; the momentum will eventually take care of itself.

Being honest with your self can be a challenge, especially if you've lived your life making the rest of the world happy. This might stir up some pretty powerful truths, and you may be tempted to talk yourself out of what you hear. Be brave. If you need help, get it. If you need to talk to a friend, grab your phone and call somebody. If you need to write it all down, start a journal. If you find you are overwhelmed, seek professional guidance to help you through this process.

Your heart is amazing; honor the truth you hear.

your turn ...

listen to your heart

What truths bubble up when you give yourself the time and space to listen to your heart? How do they make you feel? What surprises you?

2

listen to your heart

date _____

listen to your heart

2

listen to your heart

date _____

date _____

2

listen to your heart

RULE #3
feel, then decide

With a clearer head, and a focus on the heart, it becomes easier to truly feel and act on purpose rather than just react. So much of my "emotions" are really just knee-jerk reactions, reflections of how I've been trained to feel. Someone criticizes me; I am programmed to feel anger or shame. Again, someone else's rules.

Say someone cuts me off in traffic. The rule book says I have every right to get angry, let loose with a few choice words, and spend the next hour fuming. My new rule? Feel the initial feeling, and then give it a minute. Take a few deep breaths. Realize that you don't know the whole story. Maybe that driver cut me off because she is driving a sick child to the emergency room and just didn't see me there. Or, maybe she's just a selfish jerk. I'll probably never know. Either way, is it worth ruining my own day over something that really doesn't matter?

My new rule lets me decide how I truly feel. Even with the big stuff, like when someone you love says something truly hurtful, you do not have to lash out, or freak out, or crawl into a cave and want to die. You have a choice in how you handle things. Take a moment, take a breath, and then decide the best way to move forward. Don't over think this; your feelings often express themselves simply and quietly.

31

RULE #3
feel, then decide

This is not about avoiding your feelings. It's about pausing to see what's underneath those initial feelings and deciding if it serves you or not. The bonus of this approach can be fun, too. Watching other people react to your non-reaction can be priceless. Let them have the drama, mama. It has no place in my bliss.

This is also a good way to defuse someone in your life who intentionally stirs things up. I was married to someone who loved to "stir the pot" at family gatherings. He always knew the right buttons to push to trigger emotional reactions, and enjoyed seeing the results. I think maybe it was his way of gaining some control over a family dynamic that was a bit complicated.

I wonder now what would have been the result if, instead of the usual and predictable knee-jerk reactions, the other family members had paused for breath and decided on a new way of responding. Imagine the change this could make in your own circle of family and friends. The same old arguments and dramas are sure to take on an entirely new life when viewed through the lens of true feelings rather than surface emotions.

We all have triggers; dealing with them from a place of awareness and understanding leads to fewer crises and more bliss.

your turn ...

feel, then decide

What triggers you? Are you reacting true to your emotions, or out of habit or thoughtlessness? What reactions do you wish you could change? Use the space on the next few pages to jot down your thoughts.

3

feel, then decide

date _____

date _____

feel, then decide

3

feel, then decide

date _____

feel, then decide

RULE #4
focus on kindness & love

Can't find the beauty in life? Start by turning off the news and disengaging from the social drama. The constant stream of horrific news, political ranting and judgmental discussion tends to wear me down and keep me from feeling inspired, whole and powerful. I don't care what stupid things the politicians are saying, or which celebrities are getting laid or divorced, or the next crisis that may be facing the economy. I can't control any of that anyway, so why play into the chaos? And really, what impact does it have on my day right now?

I'm not suggesting you bury your head in the sand. We all have a role to play in life, and playing it with care and compassion and intelligence means being an informed citizen. Pay attention to what matters, especially when it's time to make decisions about elections, financial choices, and your family's health and well-being. Just don't dive too deep into the muck.

It's a well-understood spiritual principle that what you focus on is what you see reflected back at you. We are well trained to look for disaster and live in a state of constant anxiety. Social media especially has been carefully engineered to keep us "engaged." While it can be a good way to stay in touch with friends and family, it's clear that political and social "dialogue" has degenerated a good deal of the experience into ugliness. I won't have it anymore.

RULE #4
focus on kindness & love

I've even started to enjoy flying again. The awkward strip tease as you inch forward in line, the nervous silence as you face the TSA's x-ray vision … I just slap a big smile on my face and put out love instead of fear. If you can smile through security screening, you can smile just about anywhere.

During a recent government shut-down, when TSA agents were working without pay, I had some interesting and enlightening conversations with some of them as we waited in understaffed and over-stressed queues. Just recognizing that we are all humans, in the same place at the same time, eases the tension.

Part of being blissful is looking for and recognizing the good, no matter where you find yourself. And you can do that anywhere, any time.

your turn ...

focus on kindness & love

Do you normally look for the good in people, or expect them to disappoint you? Be honest about your usual mindset. If you tend to go negative first, you'll have a hard time finding your bliss. Look around you now. Where do you see kindness? Beauty? Love? Where can you look to find more?

date _____

4

focus on kindness & love

date _____

focus on kindness & love

4

4

focus on kindness & love

date _____

4

focus on kindness & love

RULE #5
act as if

Life has a way of putting us in places we never dreamed we'd be. For me, it all flew apart in 2009. Our tidy little plans for career advancement, building equity in our home, putting the kids through college and having a nice 401(k) on the other side evaporated before our eyes during the recession and economic upheaval. We certainly weren't alone. Those years left many people reeling, feeling as if everything they knew had vanished.

Beyond the financial upheaval, my personal life all came crashing down during one six-week period that year. Within just 42 days, my husband and I agreed that our marriage was over, my youngest graduated from high school, my oldest moved out of the nest and into her own apartment, my business partners tore our company apart (destroying my income in the process), a good friend betrayed me in a way that broke my heart, and my husband lost his job. Nothing about my world looked familiar, and I had no idea how to begin again.

It was, as my friend Bev so brilliantly put it, like someone had taken my snow globe and shaken it violently, slamming it down again and leaving me in an alien landscape.

It was my daughter Jessie who eventually helped me find my way back to good, when she signed me up for a website where you can list

RULE #5
act as if

your goals and biggest dreams. She put down one wish for me -- to live a fabulous, independent life. (If you haven't visited Tut.com and signed up for their "Notes from the Universe," take a minute and do so. It's worth it.)

For the next several months, I slowly dug my way out of the drifts and wreckage of my shattered snow globe. As much as I could, I imagined myself living that fabulous, independent life. I set up my home exactly the way I wanted, without consulting anyone. I traveled -- to Florida, to California, to Ireland, and wherever my girlfriends and I had the whim to go on a weekend road trip. I dated, something I hadn't done since I was 18. I found new clients. I threw out my old soccer mom shoes and started wearing heels again.

I acted as if the woman I dreamed of being was here in the flesh. I pictured how I would walk, talk, dress and eat, and I did just that. Mind you, I wasn't spending wildly; the divorce had let me with more debt that assets. Instead, I found myself working harder than I had in years, rebuilding my business. While money was tight, I prioritized paying down my debt and bringing in new income.

Then one miraculous day, it happened. I looked at myself and realized I WAS that woman I had imagined. I was living a fabulous, independent life!

It's much more than the old "fake it till you make it." It's about believing in the best version you have for your life, and living in a way that honors it and encourages it to materialize.

The magic lies in having clarity, a tangible vision for your life that is so vivid you can feel it. Once you are clear on what you want and why, the universe will fall all over itself to provided the hows.

your turn ...

act
as if

What's your big, juicy dream for your life? What's the image you hold of yourself at your most wonderful? What goals do you want to achieve? How will you feel when you've met them? Use the next few pages to write it down. Then begin right now acting as if it is already real.

date _____

5

act as if

date _____

date _____

5

act as if

date _____

act as if 5

RULE #6
name your fears

I strongly believe that part of the reason we accept society's rules for us, instead of creating our own, is because we often operate from fear. We have bought the myth that if we work hard, buy a house, invest wisely and play their game we end up 30 or 40 years later with enough money to buy a motor home and visit the grandkids on our way down south.

The idea of following our own path, disregarding the safe and predictable route we see all around us, is scary. Fear is a huge motivator, keeping us trapped in jobs or situations that we know aren't singing to our hearts and souls, but the idea of trying something different is terrifying. What if I fail? What if I can't do it? What if I make a mistake? What if, what if, what if...

The beautiful blessing of the 2008-2009 recession was the wake-up call so many of us received. You played by the rules and where did you end up? Underwater, unemployed, adrift in what was once a secure and safe little world. Yet even now the idea of making your own rules is often met with uncertainty and a sense of dread.

It all boils down to fear versus love. Anything that is not firmly based in love has its roots in fear. As humans we are perfectly created to amplify that fear and let it control us. We allow it to sabotage our

RULE #6
name your fears

dreams, derail our plans and justify our settling for less than we truly desire ... and deserve.

Part of me was afraid to write and publish this book. What will they think? What if it pisses someone off? What if it's just not good enough?

Then I came at if from love. What if it helps someone? What if one person hears just what they need to make a decision or change something about their life that brings them closer to the bliss they so richly deserve? Love wins. Hands down.

One thing I'm finally learning as I build my new life is this: It's always easier to slay a dragon with two (or more) swords. When you come face to face with what scares you, tell someone. Enlist the help of a friend and tell her what you're trying to do. Find a supportive group of people who want nothing but your best life for you. (And spend less time with the people who don't want to see you change because it means they might have to change to. These are the toxic ones in your life. Bless their hearts, love them, and release their hold over you.)

your turn ...

name
your fears

What fears hold you back? What scares the hell out of you and keeps you from moving forward? How would your life change if you looked at life with love, not fear? Write down your thoughts on the next few pages. Naming your fears gives you the upper hand and takes away an enormous amount of fear's power over you.

6

name your fears

date _____

6

name your fears

6

name your fears

date _____

6

name your fears

RULE #7
purge often

I'm a modern gypsy. I've had 17 moves, three of them cross-country, in my adult life. A few years back, I was packing for yet another move, this one from California to Michigan, when I realized with a jolt I had several boxes I had packed back in New York, moved to California, never unpacked, and was now planning to put them on the moving truck yet again. Was I insane?? Was I a borderline hoarder? No, I was simply following the rules I had been handed down. Maybe these resonate with you:

If your mother-in-law gave it to you, she expects to see you use it next Christmas.

If your mom gave it to you, you must keep it to give to your children.

If your children made it, you must wear it every Mother's Day until those macaroni noodles simply crumble away. (This one I still believe. I'm not heartless.)

After my divorce, I ended up with about 15% of the total household "stuff" that had accrued over my 24-year marriage. It wasn't my choice to walk away from so much of my "life," in fact I was furious about it at the time, but now I'm incredibly glad for the way it worked out. I walked away from old memories, guilty thoughts and bad habits.

RULE #7
purge often

I've moved again since, and have three simple rules when it comes to what stays in my life. I keep only what I believe is beautiful, useful or brings me joy. And I get to decide.

Even though I've now settled down and hope to stay where I am for years, I continue to purge every time I clean the house or go through a closet. And I'm firm about bringing new items into the house. I love new clothes and new shoes, and I am happy to shop for these things when I feel I need them. If I do buy something new, I am careful to get rid of at least one existing item I no longer need for every one I bring in. So I must have that new pair of brown leather boots that will look amazing when we go to Michigan in the fall? Fine, get rid of the old snowmobile boots and those torn up sandals. It's about editing ... take out the less-than-perfect to make room for the bliss.

I've discovered I can do with so much less, and my day has become simplified. Because I have less, I take better care of the things I do own. Finally, I know I can live without, let go and release the "stuff" into the universe without diminishing in any way who I am.

I've also found a blessed peace and quiet in my non-stuffed home. Even though it's a small beach cottage, here there is space to breath, to think, to meditate, to write. The more clear space I have in my life, the more space I find in my head.

your turn ...

purge often

What are you keeping that you don't want any more? Why? Jot down a few things that you don't really want to own anymore, and the feelings you get as you consider tossing them. Are those feelings valid, or based on someone else's rules?

date _____

7

purge often

date _____

purge often

date _____

7

purge often

date _____

purge often 7

RULE #8
create beauty

I believe that a huge part of why I exist is to bring beauty into the world. It's why I love to garden, and write, and decorate my home, and why I worked so hard to raise two beautiful, strong and compassionate women. Creating beauty is a passion and a purpose.

You don't have to be an artist to create more beauty in your own life. It can be a simple process of looking around and seeing what can be improved. If there is chaos, organize it. If there is dirt, clean it. If there is clutter, get rid of it. If it's dark, light a candle.

The Danish people have a wonderful word in their language. It's 'hygge' (pro-nounced 'hyooga') and it's all about embracing the art of coziness, warmth, camaraderie and beauty in your home and in your life.

The same idea holds true for your reflection in the mirror. Part of living my blissful life is recognizing my own beauty, both inside and out. Taking the time to look nice, put on my good earrings, or wrap up in a yummy scarf adds beauty to the world too. It's not about vanity, although some might argue it is. It's about offering yourself to the world in a way that reflects the juicy, vibrant feelings you get just from being you.

I recently attended a funeral for friend's mother. She was clearly loved by her family and friends, and the people in that room were in

RULE #8
create beauty

pain. I didn't know the lady, so I kept a low profile at the edge of the room, and simply let my friend know that I was there as a sign of support.

I spent a lot of time gazing at all the lovely flowers. There was nothing out of the ordinary about them; your typical funeral displays. Yet I found them incredibly vibrant and colorful. It was as if, in the midst of sadness and loss, they knew their role. Their one job was to deliver beauty to this sad event. This was their being, their entire reason for having existed. And after the funeral, their one job in this world was over. They were not worried about another flower being prettier. They didn't care what people thought when they gazed at them. They simply existed there, being their beautiful selves.

I wondered if I could be like those flowers, living my purpose without self-consciousness or conceit, self-doubt or anxiety. Could I just be, and let my own true nature speak for itself? I've learned to do this more and more, and the results are amazing.

Beauty is everywhere – especially inside of you. Let it shine.

your turn ...

create beauty

How can you bring more beauty into your life right now? What can you change, at little or no cost, that will bring more 'hygge' to your life? Do you see the beauty that's around you, or is it covered in clutter? Commit to a few ideas on the next pages on how you'll make your life a bit more beautiful.

8

create beauty

date _____

create beauty

8

create beauty

date _____

create beauty

RULE #9
make rituals

There is a certain comfort in routine. The morning cup of coffee is a perfect example. While some view it as a chore or a necessity, I see it as a beautiful ritual, a way to reconnect to the waking world.

So much of life rushes by in a blur. We find ourselves doing the same things over and over again, like dropping the kids off at school, or tossing a load of laundry into the washer. It is easy to become automated, almost unthinking, as we scurry through our lives.

This goes for the people in our lives as well. As we race the clock to get the kids on the bus, or to work on time, or to yoga class, do we even connect with the people in front of us? Do we see them, and engage with them on any authentic level, or is it all about who has to get where and when?

One way to bring more connection into my life has been through rituals. Growing up Catholic, we had plenty of rituals. Tuna noodle casserole became a Friday staple during Lent. Other times, we'd stop for donuts after Sunday Mass, which explains my ongoing craving for a good jelly bismark one day a week.

I have found new joys in recognizing and celebrating the rituals in my life. Making the bed is now an opportunity to bring my bedroom back to a state of beauty and prepare the space for another restful

RULE #9
make rituals

night.

Checking the mail gives me a minute or two to think of someone I'd like to hear from, and make plans to write or email them.

Cooking dinner moves from being a chore to celebrating a healthy offering for my body and the people who will join me at the table.

I spent a good year in what I call my black cave; not going out or being social unless forced to by well-meaning friends. Then one friend dragged me out to happy hour at the Irish pub in town. Within 15 minutes I had met some fantastic people and made some instant and long-lasting friends. I started going every Friday after work, reveling in the idea that I had a place where, like Norm, everybody knew my name. These people formed a real community with its own rituals, and welcomed me in as one of theirs. If I missed a week, someone texted or called to be sure I was okay. And I did the same if I didn't see one of my people around for a while. We celebrated holidays and special events together, and I could always find an ear to listen or a strong back to move a couch.

I no longer go to the pub every Friday; I've moved to another state and don't see that old crowd anymore. What I've learned from that experience is that we are surrounded all the time by opportunities to meet and connect with beautiful, loving people. Scientific studies have shown that, especially as we grow older, a solid community of "chosen" family is critical to being happy and avoiding depression and the other emotional problems that can afflict us. It matters.

It's our rituals, these repeated patterns of behavior, that provide a rich opportunity for connection. They give us a framework to operate within. They offer me a sense that, no matter what chaos is going on

RULE #9
make rituals

around me, I have this, and it remains good.

Recognizing the rituals that are important to your friends and family can be a wonderful way to connect.

One of the most thoughtful gifts I ever received was a coffee shop gift card that paid for several mornings of my usual latte and bagel on the way to the office. Such a simple, sweet and loving gesture. So now in addition to the coffee, I had warm thoughts of this person to go along with my breakfast ritual.

That person, whom I happened to meet at the pub one warm August evening, has since become my husband and my partner in this next round of adventure. And we still like to treat each other to lattes.

Rituals can be powerful catalysts for change and manifestation in your life. Our character is formed by our daily habits. Use with care.

your turn ...

make

rituals

What rituals do you have that are important to you? How do they help you connect with your inner self or with others? What other rituals could you develop to strengthen your sense of self and belonging? Who can you include?

date _____

9

make rituals

date _____

make rituals

9

make rituals

date _____

make rituals

RULE #10
every night, give thanks

It might seem counter-intuitive that during the darkest period of my life, I began to keep a daily gratitude journal. I remember the moment I decided to do this. It was New Year's Day, and I was picking up my 18-year-old daughter from a friend's house where she had spent the night. I was not planning to stay and socialize; in fact I had thrown on whatever I had handy and thought I could just dash in, pick her up, and get out.

Jane poured me a cup of coffee, and her son offered me waffles. I immediately declined, politely, but then it hit me. I was turning down a wonderful gift, simply because I was programmed to do so. I changed my mind, accepted, and spent a wonderful hour or so in warm companionship with her family. I needed that connection so badly that day, having spent a lonely and depressing New Year's Eve with my soon-to-be-ex-husband in the house we still shared but would soon be selling.

Being surrounded by Jane and her family was such a comfort, and it is a kindness that, while it came naturally to her, I will cherish all my life.

That night, I started journaling, documenting every blessing that I received during the day. I kept this up for a full year, and was

RULE #10
every night, give thanks

stunned by how my life began to turn around by simply recognizing the blessings all around me. The more I focused on what made me grateful, the more blessings seemed to pour forth.

As my life continued to change, and I began to manifest that "fabulous, independent life" my daughter wished for me, I got out of the habit of writing in my gratitude journal. I'm still happy, yes, and very much grateful for my life and what's in it. Yet I miss that sense of awe and wonder at just how remarkable life can be as it unfolds. So I've started journaling again, dreaming new dreams.

One of the most challenging aspects of gratitude is being grateful during the tough times. A few years ago I found myself in the emergency room with a post-surgery complication, feeling scared and horribly sick. While I huddled in the chairs alternating between freezing cold and unbearably hot, I forced myself to find things to be grateful for: the good medical care I was about to receive; the loving and concerned husband sitting next to me; even the fact that the little girl carried in by her dad was going to be seen before me.

Gratitude leads to grace, and grace is a state of bliss. Actively embrace and honor all that's good and right in your world.

your turn ...

give
thanks

What good things happened to you today? What moments of connection, affection or bliss can you recall? How about yesterday, and the day before that? Use these next few pages to write down all the good things in your life, your day, this moment. I'll start. I'm grateful to you, for reading this book and taking the risk to be vulnerable. You are beautiful and you are brave.

date _____

10

every night, give thanks

date _____

10

every night, give thanks

10

every night, give thanks

date _____

every night, give thanks

epilogue

It's been more than 10 years since my snow globe turned upside down and life became unrecognizable. And it's been eight years since I first wrote down my 10 Little Rules, that sunny October morning on m friend Laurie's back porch.

Since that time I've met some incredible people and have been honored to share my story and listen to theirs. A few of these people have become part of the growing 10 Little Rules tribe of authors, bravely sharing their own stories of life, love, loss, beauty, magic and transformation. I call them friends, sisters and partners in this growing experience we call 10 Little Rules.

No matter where you are in your own journey, buried in the drifts, shoveling out, or creating your new life, we hear you. We see you. Know that the places where you've been broken are where the light of truth comes shines through.

We are family, and you belong here.

10 LITTLE RULES
connect with our community

Stay connected to
the 10 Little Rules Community

Like and Follow our Facebook
page at facebook.com/10LittleRules
for ongoing support and discussion on
how to apply these books to living your best life.

Visit our website for updates
at www.10littlerules.com

Books in the 10 Little Rules series:
10 Little Rules for a Blissy Life by Carol Pearson
10 Little Rules for Your Creative Soul by Rita Long
10 Little Rules of Hank by Wendy Price

Watch for more 10 Little Rules books launching soon!

www.ingramcontent.com/pod-product-compliance
Lightning Source LLC
Chambersburg PA
CBHW071354090426
42738CB00012B/3121